What This Book Will Do for You

After you have finished reading this book, you will be able to write letters, memos, reports, and presentations easily and in a coherent, logical manner, using an expository style that any reader can understand, find interesting, and enjoy. Writing is not as difficult as it seems. So read on . . .

HOW TO

Write

Easily and Effectively

Donald H. Weiss

amacom
American Management Association

This book is available at a special
discount when ordered in bulk quantities.
For information, contact Special Sales Department,
AMACOM, a division of American Management Association,
135 West 50th Street, New York, NY 10020.

Library of Congress Cataloging-in-Publication Data

Weiss, Donald.
    How to write easily and effectively.

    (The Successful office skills series)
    Bibliography: p.
    Includes index.
    1. English language—Business English. I. Title.
II. Series.
PE1115.W57   1986   808'.066651   85-26739
ISBN 0-8144-7641-4

Printing number

10 9 8 7 6 5 4 3 2

CONTENTS

Introduction—
Everyone Is a Writer

Many people don't like to write. Many believe they don't know how to. Yet anyone in the business world has to write effectively; otherwise, his or her career will stall. Memos, letters, presentations—they're all expositions (that is, explanations of what something is, how to do something, or why something is the case). If you can't put together a coherent, orderly, intelligent, and interesting exposition, you can't write effectively in the business world.

So who needs lessons on how to write more effectively? Everyone. And this book will tell you how.

A Case in Point

"And so, chief," Bob Bolin summed up his report, "if we continue on the current course and add three more territories to our market each quarter, the new line will increase our gross income by 20 percent over last year."

The marketing and sales management staff of ABC Foods Company sat in silent expectation for a moment before they realized that Bob had finished his report—a report that had held their attention for 30 minutes and had included slides and charts clearly picturing the impact the new product line would have on revenues. Bob's analysis of the competition had led Phil Benson, chief of marketing operations, to quip, "If we ever let you go, Bob, you oughta take up industrial spying."

"Great presentation. Just great," Allen Bates enthused when he finally realized Bob was finished. Actually Allen, the national sales manager, was congratulating himself for having promoted Bob to new product marketing manager—in spite of the fact that no one else on the executive committee had agreed with him. Sure, nobody could match Bob's record as a sales rep and sales manager. That no one could dispute. But he was also a high school dropout, with a general equivalency diploma and only two years of college. "C'mon," Phil had taunted. "This is the big time, Allen. Bob'll never cut it."

In the end, since it was Allen's decision to make, the executive committee gave him his head. "You'll see," Allen assured them. "Bob's streetwise, tough and smart. He knows how to package what we've got to sell. He'll be O.K."

Not only did Allen feel vindicated; Bob did as well. He knew that Phil Benson didn't want him as new product marketing manager. He knew that everyone on the executive committee looked down their MBAs at him. Well, he showed them with this report. He sure did.

Phil stood up, bringing the meeting to a close merely by rising from his chair. "Bob, I liked that report. Hard-hitting. Full of the right data. The kind of stuff we need to beat the heck out of the competition. You've done your homework. Now, I'm going to have to take the hard copy with me to the board meeting next month. Have 25 copies of it sent upstairs by the thirtieth." He stopped, relighted his cigar. "Yes sir, that was all right."

As Phil exited the conference room, his staff creating a commotion as they bustled out quickly on his heels, Bob slowly lowered his 6'2", 225-pound body into the nearest chair, the terror in his eyes hardly befitting the victory he had just won.

"You O.K.?" his boss asked.

"Yeah. Sure," he answered, distracted and distant.

"Looks like that presentation took a lot out of you. But you certainly made them eat crow. Why don't you take off the rest of the day? Rest up a bit. You've earned it."

"Sure. Sounds great. Thanks." The terror had turned to anguish.

"What's the matter, Bob? You feel sick?" Allen queried, now alarmed that the stress of the presentation might have made Bob ill.

"No, I'm fine. Really. Just tired. You're right. The rest of the day off is just what the doctor ordered."

As Allen headed out the door, his back to his new product marketing manager, he heard a hoarse whisper, like a voice disembodied and floating over his head. "There is no hard copy."

He stopped. He turned slowly, but in time to see Bob's face disappear into the cup of his hands. "No hard copy?"

Bob's voice, muffled by his fingers, barely crossed the room. "No. None. I'd have been better off if I had taped it." He finally laid his hands down on the table. "I studied the data. The numbers are the easy part. The charts and slides—those were my notes. I simply talked about the data on those charts and slides." Red-rimmed eyes turned imploringly up to the better-educated man. "I can't put two English words together on paper."

"Nonsense. Anyone who can put together a report like that can write it down."

Bob shook his head. "That's why I never finished college. *D*s in English, at best."

Allen came back to the huge mahogany table and leaned forward on to it to emphasize his point. Softly but firmly he repeated himself. "Anyone who can hold his audience in the palm of his hand like that can write. Heavens, man, everyone's a writer."

You Can Write, Too

Everyone's a writer. The thought boggled Bob's mind. It boggles the minds of most average people, none of whom considers himself or herself to be proficient at one of the most basic skills of modern civilization—utilizing the written word. Throughout history, the written word has advanced human culture from a primitive, animallike existence to the exploration of outer space.

If, instead of soaring with the astronauts, you've been identifying with the abject terror that afflicted Bob when he heard the sentence Phil pronounced on him, then you need to read this book, word-for-word, sentence-for-sentence, page-for-page. Only fear itself can prevent anyone from writing if he or she can read or can make an oral presentation or both. As Allen said, "Everyone's a writer."

Some people simply write more effectively than others. They take the words that we (and every other English-speaking person) use every day, and they hang them together in such a way that you understand what they intended. They use easy-to-follow, everyday language, not stiff, archaic, or formal words. They structure their material before they write it. They're specific, to the point, and confident of what they're saying. They use active verbs and interesting adjectives. Their words fully communicate to you what they mean.

And that's the whole point of writing—to communicate fully what you mean. You get involved in the minds of effective writers because their words open their minds to you. You get involved in their emotions because their words disclose their feelings to you. You probably have never heard the names of many of the world's very effective writers because what they've written doesn't get published.

I'm not talking about undiscovered artists, misunderstood poets, or misanthropic geniuses who hide their work from the public. I'm talking about people just like yourself, many of whom communicate more effectively than some of those lucky souls who have gotten their work published. The people whose work has been published are called "authors," and the fact that they have found someone to put their words into print and sell them is all that distinguishes them from other, often equally effective, writers.

Yes, everyone's a writer. While it's true that few people possess the poetic genius of a William Shakespeare or the prose style of a C. P. Snow, every literate individual, at one time or another, writes—notes to the children, letters to parents, memos to co-workers, articles in their clubs' newsletters, presentations to the board.

That's Bob's new opportunity—a presentation to the board.

Chapter 1

Writing Is Talking on Paper

What did I say? Anyone who can speak or read English can write. That's what Allen meant when he told Bob that anyone who can make the kind of presentation he did can put it down on paper.

When writing, you send your messages through your hand rather than through your mouth. Bob even suggested that relationship when he said that he would have been better off if he had taped his presentation in advance and played it for the marketing group. However, he might have been smarter to have taped the presentation itself, because what he would have said into his tape recorder in the privacy of his office probably would not have been as effective as what he actually said during the peak moments of his talk. The presence of an audience makes a big difference.

Well, then, if when writing out something you're sitting in the privacy of your office or living room, how can you make a written communication come as alive as an oral one? The key to that mystery lies in the word *communication* itself.

The Relationship Between Speaking and Writing

Whether you're talking about speaking or about writing, you're talking about communication. You're talking about getting your ideas or your feelings out of you and transmitted to someone else. You're talking about sending a message with a content that you feel or believe in such a way that the receiver of that message can recognize what you intended to send. When you're speaking, you convey those meanings with facial expressions, body postures, and tones of voice as well as with words. You can even use the environment around you to make a point, as when Allen leaned forward on the table for emphasis.

5

Though speaking face-to-face with someone has the advantage of a complex set of elements that help complete the communication, even then people misunderstand one another, sometimes to the point of "fightin' words." Then, as you remove one or another of the elements of face-to-face communication, such as when you speak on the telephone, the opportunities for misunderstanding increase. Yet interestingly enough, the opportunities for *preventing* misunderstanding increase as well.

What I'm saying shouldn't be too new to you. You've probably often experienced a problem with getting an idea across to someone else, even when you and he or she are eyeball-to-eyeball. The more emotionally loaded the conversation—that is, the more feelings are involved—the more difficult the process becomes. Your feelings, your values, your needs, your wishes, your attitudes or biases all come into play. Meanwhile, those same characteristics in the other person come between what you're saying and what he or she hears.

On the other side of the coin, if the conversation has no emotional overtones of any kind, the communication isn't interesting enough to inspire the other person to pay attention and try to understand what you have to say. Bob's success resided in his ability to take otherwise dull facts and make them interesting to his audience. He talked about things of importance to them in a language that they understood and that excited them about what they were doing.

Bob used visual and oral devices to communicate ideas that had the same meanings and values for his audience that they had for him. That way they could interpret the messages he sent in the manner in which he intended them. If he hadn't known his audience and hadn't known what they wanted him to talk about or how they wanted him to talk about it, he would have been faced with the same problems we all experience when we try to communicate—filters, screens, and barriers that come between us and other people.

Every idea or feeling we try to get across to someone else comes out of us clothed in our own personal meanings, born in our early childhood and nurtured by our daily experiences. The language we learn may be called English, but each of us

6

learns a variety of English unique to the group in which we're raised and uniquely adapted by ourselves to ourselves. Our facial expressions, our tones of voice, our body postures—each of them has special meanings for us as well.

Now, that's not to say that there's nothing in common among our means of communicating. On the contrary, you couldn't be reading this if that were true. I'm only saying that for this information to get through to you, I have to find the proper or appropriate combination of words that (1) catch and hold your attention, (2) appeal to your personal values, and (3) have meaning for you.

I have to do that only with words—printed words, at that. And why should I distinguish between words and printed words unless that distinction were important?

Words are sounds—sounds specifically selected by our culture to designate things or to symbolize groups of things or feelings or ideas. Our range of sounds, as a basis for spoken language, makes oral communication much richer, more interesting, and more intelligible in some respects than the written representation of those sounds. Yet the written representation of those sounds gives the human being the great intellectual and emotional power that distinguishes our species from other animals.

The written representation of sounds—that's what this is all about. That's why I've expended this much energy talking about communication in general. Writing is used to represent sounds. *Writing,* as I've said, *is talking on paper.* A memo or a letter can be thought of as a one-way telephone conversation. All Bob had to do to write out his presentation was to talk to himself silently as he wrote. It's called subvocalizing.

Speaking silently helps you get the meaning you want onto the paper. For the beginning writer, speaking out loud may help even more, though it tends to slow you down. I said earlier that as you remove elements from the complex process of face-to-face speaking, you have greater opportunities to reduce misunderstanding. That's because by removing nonverbal gestures from the communication, you become more dependent upon the words you use. Listening to yourself, either subvocally or out loud, helps you become more selective in what you say and how you say it. You prepare your message with greater care. The act of writing is the end result, not the medium of the message.

As you write your memo or your letter or your presentation, you hear your message before you push it through your pen or tap it on the keys of your typewriter. You play with the words to see if they're saying what you mean to say. You listen to them as if you were your reader, and you test their meaning before you offer them up to someone else.

When writing, you're in complete control over your words. You can say the words out loud first. Listen to how they fall on your own ears, and ask yourself if they make sense. You can say the words subvocally and ask yourself if they convey the meaning you want to get across. And best of all, you can have a second chance at getting it right before sending the message on to someone else. You can have as many chances as you think necessary by rewriting what you have written.

Only the fear of writing prevents otherwise literate people from taking a chance at learning some of the mechanics of effective writing. Since writing is speaking on paper, one way to gain confidence in your ability to write is to use ordinary speech to help you write: subvocal speech at the beginning of the writing process, as I've already described, and reading out loud in the middle of the process.

Effective writers read their written products out loud in order to smooth out the rough spots before they make their final revisions. Hearing the words allows them to measure their impact better than merely seeing them. The phrasing, the tempo, the tone of the words come across more clearly. Even the logic (or illogic) of the words strikes them as they listen to the material read out loud. If a phrase seems too difficult to follow, they rewrite it. If the tenses of their verbs shift from sentence to sentence, they restate them. If their pronouns don't agree with the nouns, they rework them. They make their words do the job for which they were intended.

Effective writers also do something else before they declare the job done. They hand what they've written to another person—someone unfamiliar with what they have to say, someone whom they can trust to be honest (though fair) with them, someone who cares enough about them to give them constructive feedback. This is especially necessary if the point they are trying to make is very complex or very sophisticated or very arcane. The more removed the intended audience is from the subject matter, the more important this test becomes.

I call it the "grandma test." The name suggests that if your elderly grandma understands what you've written, anyone can. (Of course, if your "grandma" happens to have a Ph.D. in the subject matter, the test won't count.)

Effective writing comes down to this: Anyone who can talk and read can learn to write effectively, because writing is just talking on paper. It's sending your messages through your hand rather than through your mouth. The main advantage of communicating that way is that you're in full control of how those words come out—you control whether or not they're wrapped in filters that obscure their meanings and whether or not they're loaded with personal values. With the written word, you get the chance to say what you mean and to mean what you say. If your words fail to say what you intend them to say, you have only your own revisions (or lack of them) to blame.

Chapter 2

The Simple Mechanics of Effective Writing

I won't mince words. When most people think of the mechanics of writing, they think of a Mrs. Beasley waxing eloquent over the parsing of a complex sentence, of conjugating verbs, and of other *autos-da-fé* of sophomore English composition. Terrifying. Not that grammar, structure, and composition aren't important. Far be it from those of us who earn our living by writing to minimize the importance of the rules of grammar and composition for communicating ideas.

I only mean to say that, as important as they are, rules need not stand between you and writing something. As I've said, writing a memo, a letter, or a presentation is speaking on paper. We understand each other when we speak, and while we most frequently speak a fairly decent American form of English, we hardly ever think about the rules themselves. They're built into the way we learned how to speak, and the automatic following of the rules makes it *easier* to communicate with one another. It's like traffic on a busy street—keeping to the right, yielding the right of way, stopping at the red traffic signal, and so on. How could we ever get to work without those and other *commonsense* rules?

Most rules are essentially codified commonsense anyway. Likewise with writing effectively. *If writing is speaking on paper, then effective writing is speaking on paper coherently and with organization.* It's keeping your language simple and straightforward. It's making your point clear and unambiguous, using ordinary yet colorful, active language "spoken" in your own style, but in a way your audience can understand. And most of all, effective writing is being interesting, addressing issues or problems or values about which you know something and with which your audience can identify.

Speaking Coherently

Many writers babble, run off at the mouth in print. You've received letters, I'm sure, that cover the waterfront—and not just personal letters but business letters and memos as well. Seldom have so many words been used to say so little. Sometimes the recipient never does figure out the point of letters such as those.

There's no secret as to how incoherent writers do that. They just start talking about anything and everything that comes to mind. Very often these individuals fit the old image of the woebegone writer staring balefully at the blank sheet of paper in a typewriter, waiting for the muse to inspire him or

10

her to pour forth the knowledge contained within. Finally, the inspiration comes, and it comes, and it comes.

These people haven't yet learned that effective writers have worked long and hard before they sit down to write. They do the hard work before they get to the writing stage.

What have they been doing? They've been working out *what* they are going to say about the subject matter of their piece and *how* they are going to say it. They've also considered the matter of *about whom* and *for whom* they are writing. And they have considered the issues of *where* and *why* in several different ways.

Where is this piece to be read—in a business setting, in a school, in a home? Where is its action to take place? Where are the characters (if any) coming from, and to where are they going—metaphorically as well as physically?

They've not only considered why they are writing the piece; they've also considered why the reader should want to read it. They then consider why the people about whom they might be writing (real or fictional) are doing what they're doing.

Finally, they've also given thought to *when* the piece is best read. A long, complicated description of some technical procedure had best not be read too early in the day or too late in the evening unless it's heavily laced with audiovisuals that will keep the audience's eyes riveted on the screen while enlightening their minds with what they are seeing or hearing. That side of the when issue is as important as considering the when of the action in the piece, whether it be fact or fiction.

Bob's presentation contained all the basic elements of organization. At its core, the talk answered the famous six questions: what, why, where, when, who, and how. What more does a good piece of *writing* need?

Part of the answer to the question "how?" is the issue of *how you are going to write the piece.* Bob had to answer that question, too. For him, it was a matter of ordering the charts and slides in a sequence that made his point clearest, that made an impact on his audience. That's a rudimentary form of outlining.

Next to learning how to speak, how to outline one's thoughts into a logical and/or chronological order has to be the most important tool of ordinary communication.

Though the thought of using the rules of grammar frightens many people, they don't realize that they use them all the time. The rules reflect how people do, in fact, communicate with one another effectively. Even the argot of the streets has its own grammatical forms.

The rules of grammar are nothing more than an outline, a way to organize words into patterns that unify one person's intention with another person's interpretation. And contrary to the bugaboos created by early-childhood teachers, the rules are not inflexible, rigid, and elitist. They bend with the times and with the people. They bend, but they don't break apart or become something wholly other than what they were. Though in a later section I'll work on the effective *use* of words ("diction"), I won't get into lessons in grammar.

I mention the rules of grammar only because they form a basic element in the organization of any form of communication—oral or written. I mention it only to point out that most of us grew up using the rules, whether we knew it or not. Most of us speak in grammatically correct simple sentences, sometimes grammatically correct compound or complex sentences. We use nouns, verbs, adjectives, and adverbs, placed in the appropriate sequence of subject and predicate—and we never stop to think about it.

It's when we do stop to think about it that we become self-conscious and frightened. It's like trying to *tell*—not show—someone how to tie his or her shoelaces. Try it. See what I mean.

But that's exactly what an effective writer does. He or she becomes self-conscious about the rules, at least when starting out to become an effective writer. That doesn't mean having to go back to school. That merely means getting a hold of a good style manual or writing guide that can clarify such ideas as the agreement of subject and verb, nouns and pronouns; the effective use of adverbs or adjectives; the relationship between verbs and objects; and so on. This, by the way, is not such a book.

No, the outlines with which I want to deal here are those that help you focus your ideas. I'm going to assume that you can handle sentences. I'm concerned with the coherence among sentences rather than among individual words. To accomplish my objectives, I'll talk about sequencing ideas into an exposition, into a narration, or into a description (or some combination of all of them).

Exposition—Telling What, Why, or How

The most commonly used form of communication is exposition—what the college textbooks call expository writing. We use this form primarily to tell other people something—by presenting facts, giving directions, recording events, interpreting facts or events, or developing opinions and/or beliefs. Almost all business letters or memos, as well as Bob's presentation, are expository.

Most ordinary conversations are expository as well. Many elements of imaginative fiction are expository, as when the author's voice presents facts about his or her scenes or characters. Exposition is not some special style of writing but rather an integral part of our ordinary communication.

Now, to make his communication coherent, Bob took his charts and slides and sequenced them to describe the new product, to describe the relationship of the new product to the products of ABC's competitors, to explain how to package the new product and how to open new territories with it, and then he interpreted how all that would translate into increased revenues. By sequencing his ideas, he outlined his presentation.

(By the way, I'll stick with Bob throughout this book to illustrate how you can tighten up anything you write and make it effective. Keep in mind the expository nature of a one-page letter or a memo. Everything I say about writing Bob's presentation applies to them as well. From this point on, I'm hitting on that 90 percent of the work that's done between the time you take on an assignment or make a decision to write a letter or a memo and the time you actually begin writing the piece. As I develop the stages of the writing process, think of something on which you can work as we go along. Every time I have Bob go through one stage or another, you should copy the approach, using your own subject matter and your own format.)

Bob's been given an assignment—to "make hard copy" out of his presentation. To do that he need only follow his own instincts, using the same sequence of ideas.

Chapter 3

How to Develop Your Ideas Successfully

Let Your Ideas Flow

One simple method for sequencing ideas begins with your jotting down all of them without any concern for sequence. Just dump your mind out onto a piece of paper. Don't worry about grammar; don't concern yourself with logical order. Those come late in the process, when you evaluate and organize the ideas you're dumping onto the paper.

Just make a list of ideas as they surface. Or to use psychologists' jargon—freely associate.

To be sure, there must first be something in there to dump. Bob's success depended on his knowledge of his subject matter. He researched the company's new product, the marketplace, and everything else he needed to know about what would happen if he introduced his product one way rather than another. With those data in mind, he set about putting together the visuals, from which he was able to speak to his also knowledgeable audience.

Armed with information, you're able to let the ideas flow. In the accompanying sidebar (Idea Sheet 1), I've simulated a free flow of ideas that might have come from the mind of Bob

Idea Sheet 1

Whole-grain cereals. No sugars, addatives, preservatives, no junk.

Adult food

High energy potential   Like Total, Quaker Oats

packaged for adults   Muted colors

Image of health, wholesomeness

Not too artey, no landscape pix

But sports. It's not Wheaties

Hit the shelves in early spring, focus on getting ready for
summer—slimming down, trimming up.

Redevelop product after three years

Winter campaign aims at protection against winter colds.

Positive campaign, no attacks on the competition.

Reclosable box for maintaining freshness. Does double
duty. Reinforces the wholesomeness Idea—keep it
fresh, keep it nutritious—and makes storage easier

Priced under competition by 2% for first three months of
opening a territory; raise price to competitive level after
a 20% market share achieved.

Name. Reserve three product names. Test 3 different
packages in slightly different marketplaces.

Focus on the benefits of eating   Positive campaigns

- -

Bolin as he prepared to produce hard copy for Phil to take to the board meeting. Take a look at what a jumble an "idea sheet" can be. When you've finished reading the notes I set down in Bob's name, return to this page and read on.

That's enough. I've jotted down a sufficient number of notes to illustrate my point. I don't have to design Bob's entire new-product campaign to do that.

As you can see, the sheet is just a jumble of ideas— brainstorming with pencil and paper. There's no order to it. Some words are misspelled; others are left out. There's no concern for grammar or punctuation. *It's purpose is to get everything out*—even if it's irrelevant and finally discarded.

The first thing for Bob to do is to reread those notes, to see if he can think of anything else to say. Having decided that he's dumped as much as he can for now, he can begin massaging it. For example, he can insert the missing word *not* in the idea "But not sports." He can eliminate redundancies or repetitions, as in "Positive campaigns."

Devise a Statement of Purpose

Peek at the revised version of Idea Sheet 1, in the accompanying sidebar. It shows how Bob begins to put some order into his thinking. Then return to this page to continue your reading.

As you can see, the first step consists of identifying simple things to reduce some of the clutter. Once you've completed that step, it's time to put the pencil into high gear. Now you perform literary "surgery" to get your ideas in order.

This surgery begins with your deciding why you're performing it in the first place. What is the purpose of writing up this presentation? For Bob, it's to explain to the board of directors, none of whom is as knowledgeable as Phil and his staff, why ABC Foods is introducing a new breakfast cereal and how it will increase revenues. Well, now that he has a purpose, he knows what he needs to talk about.

The statement of purpose (the goal) specifies what the audience needs to or wants to know as well as what you need to or want to tell it. Properly written, the statement of purpose also contains the basic thesis of the presentation—

Revised Idea Sheet 1

Whole-grain cereals. No sugars, add~~a~~itives, preservatives, no junk.

Adult food

High energy potential   Like Total, Quaker Oats

packaged for adults   Muted colors

Image of health, wholesomeness

Not too artey, no landscape pix

not
But~~s~~ports. It's not Wheaties

Hit the shelves in early spring, focus on getting ready for summer—slimming down, trimming up.

Redevelop product after three years

Winter campaign aims at protection against winter colds.

Positive campaign, no attacks on the competition.

Reclosable box for maintaining freshness. Does double duly. Reinforces the wholesomeness idea—keep it fresh, keep it nutritious—and makes storage easier

Priced under competition by 2% for first three months of opening a territory; raise price to competitive level after a 20% market share achieved.

Name. Reserve three product names. Test 3 different packages in slightly different marketplaces.

Focus on the benefits of eating   ~~Positive campaigns~~

---

in Bob's case, "The introduction of a new product will increase revenues."

Now consider what the statement of the thesis does. It demands that anything Bob has to say in some way describe, support, illustrate, demonstrate, or explain that statement. It forces him to conform his ideas to a set of topics that clearly relate to the thesis.

You may be wondering why I had Bob do the brainstorming first. Why didn't I have Bob use this statement of purpose and/or the thesis to focus his thinking from the outset?

I deliberately waited until now in order to encourage creativity and innovation. Before brainstorming, whether on paper or in a group, set no limits on what to consider. Bring forward as much information as you may have stored away in your mind. There will be time enough later to haul out the scissors and paste and rework your ideas into final form.

Here's where Idea Sheet 2, in the accompanying sidebar, comes in. Just as he did with the first idea sheet, Bob simply lets his mind run free, producing a list of categories that he knows from past experience and training he will need to cover in order to describe, explain, and support his thesis—areas he must touch on in order to flesh out his presentation. Without all that, he won't achieve his ultimate purpose.

Look at Idea Sheet 2 now before reading on.

- -

Idea Sheet 2

Areas to Cover in the Presentation

Purpose of the presentation: To explain why ABC Foods is introducing a new breakfast cereal and how it will increase revenues.

1. What—product:

2. Who and why—target population:

3. What—image:

4. Who—competition:

5. What and why (how)—packaging:

6. What and why (how)—pricing:

7. When to enter the market:

8. Where to enter the market:

- - - - - - - - - - - - - - - - - - - -

As you can see, Bob considers all of the five Ws—what, why, when, who, where—as well as how. He ties them to randomly selected but specific aspects of what he thinks should go into the marketing plan of a new product. That way, the outcome of the idea sheet consists of a list of topics from which he can develop his thesis. To make that list complete, he'll have to combine Revised Idea Sheet 1 and Idea Sheet 2. That combination will then become Amended Idea Sheet 2.

The function of Amended Idea Sheet 2 is to identify the relevancy of Bob's ideas to his purpose. With this combined sheet, he identifies whether or not he has been as thorough as possible up to this point. He also searches for contradictions between ideas and eliminates them. He looks for overlapping ideas. He seeks out connections between ideas that will later help him to set up his topic outline. And finally, he discovers here what other research he has to do before he can finish the presentation.

Starting with Revised Idea Sheet 1, he marks each idea with at least one number of a category on Idea Sheet 2. He does this simply by asking, "Which area (or areas) that I have to cover does this idea address?" Or simply, "Where does this idea fit?" Bob recognizes that "Redevelop product after three years" doesn't fit—it doesn't conform to a topic related to either his purpose or his thesis. He deletes it.

He finds other nonconformities as well, which I'll go into after you look at how Bob labeled the items he had listed on Revised Idea Sheet 1. Take a look at Amended Idea Sheet 1, in the accompanying sidebar. Return to this point when you're finished.

Just by running your finger down the margin of Amended Idea Sheet 1, you probably noticed that Bob left some gaps. Those gaps will become painfully obvious to him as soon as he enters those items in his list on Idea Sheet 2. Now you'll see why the spaces were left between the category headings on Idea Sheet 2.

Look at Amended Idea Sheet 2, in the sidebar on page 22, before continuing with your reading here.

The irrelevancy and the repetition are noticeable by their absence. Bob eliminated them once he organized his ideas

Amended Idea Sheet 1

1 Whole-grain cereals. No sugars, additives, preservatives, no junk.

2 Adult food

3 High energy potential   Like Total, Quaker Oats

5 packaged for adults   Muted colors

3 Image of health, wholesomeness

3 Not too artsy, no landscape pix

3 But not sports.   It's not Wheaties

7 Hit the shelves in early spring, focus on getting ready for summer—slimming down, trimming up.

Redevelop product after three years

7 Winter campaign aims at protection against winter colds.

3 Positive campaign, no attacks on the competition.

5 Reclosable box for maintaining freshness. Does double duty. Reinforces the wholesomeness idea—keep it fresh, keep it nutritious—and makes storage easier

6 Priced under competition by 2% for first three months of opening a territory; raise price to competitive level after a 20% market share achieved.

5 Name. Reserve three product names. Test 3 different packages in slightly different marketplaces.

3 Focus on the benefits of eating   ~~Positive campaigns.~~

Amended Idea Sheet 2

Areas to Cover in the Presentation

Purpose of the presentation: To explain why ABC Foods is introducing a new breakfast cereal and how it will increase revenues.

1. What—product: Whole-grain cereals. No sugars, additives, preservatives, no junk.
2. Who and why—target population: Adult food
3. What—image: High energy potential   Like Total, Quaker Oats   Image of health, wholesomeness   Not too arty, no landscape pix   But not sports. Positive campaign, no attacks on the competition. Focus on the benefits of eating.
4. Who—competition: Total   Quaker Oats   Wheaties
5. What and why (how)—packaging: packaged for adults Muted colors   Reclosable box for maintaining freshness. Does double duty. Reinforces the wholesomeness idea— keep it fresh, keep it nutritious—and makes storage easier. Name. Reserve three product names. Test 3 different packages in slightly different marketplaces.
6. What and why (how)—pricing: Priced under competition by 2% for first three months of opening a territory; raise price to competitive level after a 20% market share achieved.
7. When to enter the market: Hit the shelves in early spring, focus on getting ready for summer—slimming down, trimming up. Winter campaign aims at protection against winter colds.
8. Where to enter the market:

----

by topic. He also noticed that he didn't address topic 8: "Where to enter the market." Nothing's in that space.

It doesn't take much to see that he has far too little information concerning the competition. And for all his comments about image and packaging, he has very few specifics and too many negatives. It's nearly impossible to develop a positive-image campaign on the few words he's generated under the "What—product" heading.

Now he knows what work is cut out for him. He needs to do some additional research on the competition; he needs to develop a list of positive adjectives to describe the new cereal; and so on.

As Bob puts this material together, he begins to realize that as good as his oral presentation was, he might have made it even better if he had approached it this way. Phil expected that the presentation had been backed up by something in writing. The most effective oral presentations are. That Bob didn't have at least a written outline would have taken Phil completely by surprise.

Bob is ready to put together his preliminary outline once he fleshes out the ideas he includes under each category. Obviously, since I'm merely using this situation to illustrate the development process, I won't put together a completed Idea Sheet 2. Instead, let's turn now to the outline itself.

Chapter 4

The Topic Outline— Building a Framework for Your Ideas

Few people ever go through the steps described in the previous chapter. Surprisingly few people ever bother to write an outline, and most college students usually write their outlines after they've finished their essays. Why people want to make writing so difficult confounds me.

The outline, probably the most critical part of the writing

process, is the skeleton on which to hang the piece's flesh. Especially if you use both a topic outline and a sentence outline, you finish nearly half the writing itself before you begin.

Here, I'll talk only about the topic outline. In the next chapter, I'll discuss the use of a sentence outline to expand on the topic outline. (As you gain experience with outlining, you'll find yourself skipping one outline or the other, using whichever approach is more comfortable for you. This book was built directly from a sentence outline, without the intermediate step of a topic outline.)

The Purpose of a Topic Outline

First, what can an outline do for you? I talked briefly earlier about sequencing. That's one thing. But that sequencing comes from still another value of a topic outline—direction or focus. Effective writers know "who dunnit" long before they get to the last page. Their outline tells them how the story's going to end. It tells them before they get started writing.

I'll backtrack a few pages to explain that. Remember I said that the statement of purpose, if written properly, identifies the main point of the piece—its thesis? If I repeat the purpose of Bob's presentation, you'll immediately recall what I'm talking about: "To explain why ABC Foods is introducing a new breakfast cereal and how it will increase revenues."

That clearly shows the main point of Bob's thesis: *By introducing a new breakfast cereal, ABC Foods can increase revenues.*

That's what Bob's piece is all about. That's what the presentation must describe, explain, and demonstrate. Whether he makes that statement at the beginning, in the middle, or at the end, unless Bob tells his audience that point, they might never get the gist of what he's saying.

When making a presentation, whether orally or in writing, you have to use the "Tell 'em" principle:

> *Tell 'em what you're going to tell 'em.*
> *Tell 'em.*
> *Tell 'em what you've told 'em.*

At the start of this book, I stated the learning objectives I hoped to help you achieve. I told you what I was going to tell you. I've been telling you, and in each chapter I start by telling you what I'm going to tell you in that chapter. And at the end, I'll tell you what I told you—I'll summarize the whole book. The "Tell 'em" principle—it's one of those communication devices that separates the bumbling writers from the effective ones.

The topic outline forces you to use the "Tell 'em" principle. It begins with the thesis, which I will develop in just a moment, and it ends with a summary of the topics listed in the body of the outline. As you'll see, it is the "Tell 'em" principle in action.

The Thesis Sentence

The thesis—maybe I should shout it: *THE THESIS*—tells 'em what you're going to tell 'em. It consists of your main point, your point of view, the position you're taking, the reasons for taking it. I'll illustrate it first and then briefly discuss each element. Bob's thesis will ultimately read:

By introducing All Grains Breakfast Cereal, we can increase revenues by 20 percent over last year if we make inroads in the market shares of the competition; if we target an adult, physical fitness–oriented market; if we develop a comprehensive marketing strategy; and if we time our campaigns and market penetration properly.

Bob's main point is that "we can increase revenues by 20 percent over last year." That's the *what* of the thesis sentence. It also implicitly expresses his point of view—that it's a good idea to increase revenues by 20 percent. That implicit judgment shines a light of benediction on all the rest of the sentence because, logically, if it is good to increase revenues and if those steps he lists will increase revenues, then they are good also.

Just for a moment, let's look at the real power of the thesis sentence by expressing a counterthesis—a point of view contrary to Bob's. For example, "We need to increase revenues by 20 percent over last year, but introducing All Grains

Breakfast Cereal will not be successful because . . ." Everything after "because" then supports the viewpoint that the new product won't do what's needed.

The new statement expresses the same value as Bob's statement—raising revenues is good—but then it goes on to say that Bob's suggestion is not good. The difference rests in what I call *the main point as opposed to the point of view.* The main point in the second sentence is not that ABC Foods needs to raise revenues but rather that Bob's suggestion won't work.

Now you see why taking the time to write out a thesis sentence is as important as it is: *to prevent confusing your main point with your point of view. The one is usually a matter of fact or of opinion or of belief; the other is usually the expression of a value or a judgment about the matter of fact, opinion, or belief.*

People often get wrapped up in the "filters" created by points of view. They then lose sight of their main point in the process. An appropriately written thesis sentence prevents that from happening.

When first getting used to writing theses, it's to your advantage to state the main point first.

Main Point: we can increase revenues by 20 percent over last year

Then, list the documentation, the explanation, the description, or whatever else goes into the balance of your thesis sentence. I'll call it, for want of a better name, the justification.

Justification: by introducing All Grains Breakfast Cereal . . .

Now Bob can go to work with his what, who, where, when, why, and how. Each element in the justification comes from the Amended (and complete) Idea Sheet 2. That justification is then turned into another list of topics—the list of what Bob's going to tell 'em.

Sequencing and the Principle of Selection

Here's where sequencing begins, and once more you have to consider *how* you're going to organize the topics. You need a principle of selection that will help you decide what to dwell on, in what order to dwell on it, in what aspect(s) you can afford to use emotional impact, and in what aspect(s) you have to eliminate emotional impact ("Nothin' but the facts, ma'am").

I said earlier that the thesis sentence shown in the previous section *ultimately* reads that way. That implies that it took some work to get it into its present shape. If you'll recall, Idea Sheet 2 listed the topics at random. However, before getting the final topic outline to look the way he wanted it to, Bob had to arrange and rearrange the order, or sequence, of the topics themselves. That's the function of a principle of selection.

A principle of selection enables you to ask pertinent questions, just as was done with Idea Sheet 2 when you eliminated irrelevancies by asking "Does it fit?" Now you ask a different set of questions, the answers to which will settle the issues of importance, value, impact, meaning, logic, or chronology.

One reason I used the word *justification* to refer to the second part of the thesis sentence is that chronological ordering of events may not give you what you need. For Bob to have organized his presentation according to a list of when certain steps in the marketing plan will occur would have been to lose sight of the fact that he has to argue in favor of his plan for raising revenues. Therefore, his principle of selection has to emphasize those topics that will support his argument.

He could consider importance to be his main principle. How important is this information to my main point? Can I communicate my main point or fulfill my purpose without this information or if I downplay it? How important is this information to the reader? How important is the point of view to the information, or how much emotional loading should I put into the language? Answers to those questions would tell Bob where he should place each topic and how much space he should devote to it.

To illustrate this point another way—I made a decision at the outset of this book that coherence is the most important aspect of effective writing. I've devoted a great deal of space to this topic of coherence because I believe that outlining gives you the coherence you need to become an effective writer.

In short, I asked the question, as my own principle of selection, "What will help anyone who can speak and read in English to become a more effective writer?" I answered the question in several ways and then asked, "What is the most important topic of all?" And now you're reading it.

Another criterion for organizing your material is whether or not your topics explain the meaning of your main point or of your point of view. Do they clarify the issues? Do they settle the issues? Do they help the reader understand what you intend him or her to receive from you? For example, you'll notice in Bob's outline (see Outline Format 1, presented at the end of the chapter) a topic called, "How All Grains Breakfast Cereal differs from the competition's products." He is trying to head off the question, "Why should we enter this new market? What do we have to offer that the competition cannot match or beat?"

A third criterion for deciding on sequencing or deciding the extent to which to dwell on a topic is the value of the material to your main point. This criterion differs from importance in that the criterion of importance refers to how dependent the main point is on the information, whereas value refers to the degree to which the information enhances or elaborates on the main point or on the other information in the piece. Bob's conclusions are important to his main point; he can't make his point without them. His statistical charts and tables add value insofar as they clarify or illustrate his conclusions. They demonstrate the logic of his conclusions as well.

The logic of an outline takes several forms. First, its logic refers to what I just said: The topics internal to the outline demonstrate the soundness of the reasoning and the conclusions drawn. Second, I refer to the logic of the topical arrangement itself.

In order for what you're going to tell 'em to make sense, you may have to tell 'em in a sequence that enables your readers to draw a conclusion from a series of propositions. You may make inferences from assumptions about or facts regarding your topic, and the conclusions are the logical consequences of those assumptions (deductive reasoning). This is done all the time in scientific or quasi-scientific writing, especially where a great deal of math is involved. Or you can reason from data about your subject matter, as when describing the correlations between cancer and tobacco use, and so forth (inductive reasoning).

In either case, your thesis sentence, stated up front, explains what you intend to try to prove. Your summary, at the end, explains how you think you proved your main point or supported your point of view.

As you can see from what I've been saying, the most frequently used principle of selection, chronology, may not be the most satisfactory way to communicate what you want to say to someone else. The sequence in which something happened becomes important only where the main point or the point of view demands a historical account.

To decide the importance of chronology, you need only ask, Why would the history of this subject be important to the reader? Of what value would it be to my main point or point of view? How does it explain what I'm attempting to say? How does it advance the logic of my argument or the logical structure of my piece? And finally, what impact would it have on the reader?

Considerations of Emotional Loading

The impact of anything you put in your piece refers to what I earlier called the emotional loading of the words. Words not only denote things, people, places, or events; they also symbolize what are called abstract concepts—the most significant abstract concepts being love, hate, peace, trust, truth, beauty, and so forth. When writing your outline, you have to keep in mind what impact those words or concepts will have on your readers.

Abstract concepts have connotations loaded with emotional values. Your nouns, the words I just listed above, your adjectives, and your adverbs carry much of the emotional tone of your piece—really important; a lovely, sunny day; an awe-inspiring experience; a work of great beauty. Verbs,

29

however, have the greatest impact on the reader. They convey the action. They describe the situation. Compare the two sentences below and see what I mean.

Our market population is the adult physical-fitness group, between the ages of 21 and 35.
We'll attempt to capture the adult physical-fitness market, between the ages of 21 and 35.

Even without elaborating on the point, you can see the importance of it through the phrase "attempt to capture" as opposed to "our market population is." The verb *to be* is static; it describes rather than illustrates the idea. In Chapter 6, I'll talk about "diction" (the effective use of words) and give you some tips on building your vocabulary of colorful or active words.

Here I'm concerned with the issue of what to place where in the outline, and as you consider those emotional values, you have to decide whether what you say or how you say it will excite the reader to continue on past that point. You have to consider whether or not what you say or how you say it will turn off the reader, make him or her put your piece aside.

Other considerations of emotional loading get more complicated than that. The connotations of words substitute for tones of voice, facial expressions, and other nonverbal gestures and help make the mental image you want your reader to have more vivid. Remember, the environment in which you're attempting to communicate is incomplete.

Your outline should take into consideration what would grab the reader's attention rapidly, hold his or her attention throughout the piece, and enable the reader to identify with the situation or agree with your main point or your point of view. I deliberately invented Bob's plight as a way of capturing your attention and giving you someone with whose agony you could empathize. His writing requirements then provide me with continuity and illustrative materials.

And so, I've tried to show why the skeleton is so important to the piece, and I've tried to show you how to build one. *I can summarize the point with the old cliché that every story has a beginning, middle, and end.* The topic outline lets you organize your materials into that standard format. It shows you what you're going to tell 'em, how you're going to tell 'em, and why you're going to tell 'em certain things rather than or before other things.

The Topic Outline Format

Now, before I ask you to take a look at Bob's topic outline, I need to make one observation about an outline itself. Each of the parts of an outline must be divisible by at least two, unless it's not divisible at all. That means simply that any time you subdivide a topic, you have to have at least two subtopics or your topic is not divisible at all. Look at this illustration (shown first in an incorrect format):

I. Introducing All Grains Breakfast Cereal
   A. What it is
II. Underselling the competition and capturing our share of the market

Now a correct format:

I. Introducing All Grains Breakfast Cereal
   A. What it is
   B. How eating it benefits an adult
II. Underselling the competition and capturing our share of the market

Multiple subdivisions underscore the complexity of the idea in the topic. Every roman numeral represents a major division of the piece. Every subdivision represents a significant part of that division. In a very short piece, each roman numeral is a new paragraph, the topic itself being the main point of what is called the topic sentence of the paragraph (which I'll discuss in more detail in the section of the next chapter dealing with sentence outlines). In a long piece, each roman numeral represents a section or a chapter or a unit, and each capital letter contains the topics of each new paragraph.

The more you subdivide your material, the easier it becomes to write the piece. You're building your paragraphs right there in the skeleton of what you're writing. To produce the finished product, you hang the flesh on the bones, then you dress it up with your revisions.

That cliché about the beginning, middle, and end—as a summary statement—really doesn't do justice to this extensive portion of the book. Instead, I'll summarize this section by producing a complete topic outline (Outline Format 1) for Bob's presentation.

Don't get hung up on the specifics of the presentation; I'm merely inventing them for the purpose of the present discussion. Rather, look for these crucial features:

1. What is Bob's main point?
2. How has he used his justification to organize his material or topics?
3. What principle of selection do you think he has used as his primary criterion? What other criteria do you think he has used?

After you've studied the topic outline, turn to the next chapter.

- -

Outline Format 1

Thesis: By introducing All Grains Breakfast Cereal, we can increase revenues by 20 percent over last year if we make inroads in the market shares of the competition; if we target an adult, physical fitness–oriented market; if we develop a comprehensive marketing strategy; and if we time our campaigns and market penetration properly.

I. Introducing All Grains Breakfast Cereal
    A. What it is
    B. How eating it benefits an adult
II. Making inroads into the market shares of the competition
    A. Our main competitors and their market shares
        1. General Mills (XX%)
        2. General Foods (XX%)

3. Kellogg's (XX%)
4. Quaker Oats (XX%)
5. Carnation (XX%)
- B. How All Grains Breakfast Cereal differs from the competition's products
  1. Additives
  2. Sugar and sodium
  3. Recommended daily allowances
- C. Competitors' marketing strategies
  1. Pricing
  2. Image and packaging

III. Target population: physical fitness—oriented adults
- A. Young adults—singles and marrieds—ages 21–35
- B. Parents of young children
- C. Senior citizens with health concerns

IV. A comprehensive marketing strategy
- A. Image—to build on fitness and health consciousness of adults
  1. Nutrition issues
  2. Weight control
  3. Fiber and bulk
- B. Training children for good nutrition habits
- C. Buy-now incentives for rapid penetration
  1. Underselling the competition by 2%
  2. Coupons for future purchases

V. Timing of campaigns and market penetration
- A. Spring campaign
  1. Tied to fitness
  2. Tied to slenderizing for beachwear
- B. Coastal regions first
  1. More adventuresome markets for tryout effort
  2. High concentrations of target populations
- C. Winter campaign
  1. Will capitalize on severe weather conditions of interior regions
  2. Tied in to nutrition to prevent winter colds
- D. Timed sequence for entering other regions

- -

Chapter 5

Creating a Finished Piece of Writing from Your Framework

The topic outline possesses power. No doubt about it. It directs your entire effort and gives you the skeleton from which you will develop your written piece. Yet its power is limited, as you could see from Bob's outline in the previous chapter. The bones of the skeleton are all incomplete, or fragment, sentences.

You still have to flesh out the finished product to drive home your message and convince your audience of the rightness of your main point or your point of view. That takes complete sentences and colorful or active language to succeed. As promised, this is where I'll discuss sentence outlines and drafts.

The Sentence Outline—The First Layer

In order for that woebegone writer staring at a blank sheet of paper to prevent so-called writer's block, he or she needs idea sheets and Outline Format 1. When you know in advance what you intend to write about and how to write about it, you produce something worthwhile after every bout with the typewriter or word processor. With a sentence outline (called Outline Format 2), your productivity will increase immeasurably. Here's why.

When you write a sentence outline, you take each topic in Outline Format 1 and turn it into at least a simple sentence—a subject and a predicate. Each major subdivision represents a significant part of the piece—let's say, in this case, that each roman numeral represents a paragraph in Bob's presentation. Each capital letter represents an essential sentence in the paragraph, and each arabic number represents elements of those sentences or additional sentences in the paragraph. In short, as you flesh out your topic outline into a sentence outline, you're *writing* your piece. (Well, at least you're writing the basic elements of your first draft.)

I'll use roman numeral I of Bob's topic outline to illustrate Outline Format 2, a sentence outline, in the accompanying sidebar. I'll treat it as a short paragraph, and again, don't be distracted by the details. I'm really not trying to sell cereal.

Outline Format 2

I. By introducing All Grains Breakfast Cereal, we can increase revenues by 20 percent over last year.
   A. All Grains Breakfast Cereal is a multigrain cereal with unbleached, cracked wheat as its main ingredient.
   B. High in protein, it provides more lasting energy than do sugar-coated or corn-based cereals.

If Bob has nothing more to say about All Grains Breakfast Cereal, the first draft of that paragraph *is written.* If he wants to elaborate on any of the sentences (or all of them), he need only insert the additional material as he writes his next draft. The sentence outline, then, because it contains your thesis sentence and because you can convert each topic in the justification into the crucial concept of the paragraph (the topic sentence), can be used as the first draft of a short piece.

It can also be used as an entire memo. I'll reword Bob's thesis and roman numeral I to illustrate how outlining can turn the most ordinary subject matter into a most outstanding memo. Read the excerpt from Bob's memo to Phil, in the sidebar on page 36, before moving on.

The First Draft—The Second Layer

Whether you use your sentence outline as your first draft or write out a draft in addition to it, you should expect to have to

Memorandum

To: Phil Benson
          Chief of Marketing Operations

From: Bob Bolin
          New Product Marketing Manager

Subject: All Grains Campaign

Date: December 10, 1986

During the coming year, ABC Foods will make a bold entrance into the adult breakfast cereal market, with a projected impact of a 20 percent increase in revenues over the last fiscal year. We will do this by introducing All Grains Breakfast Cereal, the morning meal for physical fitness–conscious adults. The campaign will have its greatest success if we develop a comprehensive marketing strategy and if we time our campaigns and market penetration properly.

All Grains Breakfast Cereal is a multigrain cereal with unbleached, cracked wheat as its main ingredient. High in protein, it provides more lasting energy than do sugar-coated or corn-based cereals. Our first priority when marketing All Grains is to make inroads into the market shares of our main competitors: General Mills (XX percent), General Foods (XX percent), Kellogg's (XX percent), Quaker Oats (XX percent), Carnation (XX percent). To impact those markets, we need to show how our product differs from theirs.

Our campaign will emphasize our pledge of no additives (that includes sugar and sodium)—a truly healthful product. We will also draw attention to the proven balance of vitamins and minerals that meet or exceed recommended daily allowances . . .

massage the material at least one more time before you send it for final typing. The first draft is only the flesh on the bones.

In an ordinary, everyday, garden-variety piece of expository writing, such as Bob's presentation, you use your thesis sentence as the heart of your introduction. That's how you tell your readers, up front, what you're going to tell 'em. The rest of the draft follows the outline.

If you've done all your preliminary work carefully and thoughtfully, you need only work step-by-step from beginning to end. On the other hand, as you develop your first draft, you may decide to restructure a part of the outline or delete something or add an important point you didn't think of before. Don't be afraid to make your change(s). After all, you've written the outline on paper, not in concrete.

At the same time, your alterations must conform to the thesis sentence's main point and can't contradict anything in the justification that you've already written. One way to guarantee that the changes haven't disrupted the flow and connection of all the outline's parts is to use the sentences with the roman numerals for building a summary statement at the end of the sentence outline or at the end of the first draft. If the summary statement doesn't look like the thesis sentence, then something went wrong during the writing, and you have to go in to make things right.

That's the first revision—putting the flesh on the bones. The second revision puts the clothing on the flesh.

Chapter 6

Adding Color, Excitement, and Style to Your Writing

Bob's thesis sentence as stated in his outline left a lot to be desired. It had no punch, no pizzazz. It didn't do anything to grab the reader's attention and hold it. As originally written, it was merely a working tool. To add zing, I rewrote it in the memo you read earlier.

During the coming year, ABC Foods will make a bold entrance into the adult breakfast cereal market, with a projected impact of a 20 percent increase in revenues over the last fiscal year. We will do this by introducing All Grains Breakfast Cereal, the morning meal for physical fitness–conscious adults. The campaign will have its greatest success if we develop a comprehensive marketing strategy and if we time our campaigns and market penetration properly.

You get the idea—color, action. "ABC Foods will make a bold entrance . . ." At the same time, it's simple and straightforward.

Diction—Dressing Up the Flesh

Diction in writing has nothing to do with pronunciation. It refers to the way in which you choose your words. Very few things in human experience limit you to the use of one and only one word to describe or explain them. Nothing binds you to the choice of one word rather than another except the degree of effectiveness or precision or appropriateness of the word you choose for conveying your meaning. A good synonym dictionary or thesaurus is a must for any writer's library.

No rules govern the choice of words, but there are some guidelines that will help you sort through the thousands of words in our language to choose what for you will be the most effective words at the time you write them.

First, good diction means that your *readers* find the words well chosen to convey your meanings or attitudes or values or beliefs or opinions. Faulty diction means that your readers' expectations haven't been met in some way; they don't understand what you've written or can't empathize with the point of view. (They don't have to agree with you to empathize; they must merely feel you have a right to say what you've written.)

Now you see why I said very early on in this book that

effective writers give their work the "grandma test." *You* usually know what you mean when you write something. For that reason, you read your piece with a preconceived notion of what's supposed to be there and what you intended by what's there. Your mind fills in gaps created by missing words or by missing ideas that should have been developed at some point. You *filter in* what isn't there.

Likewise, you *filter out* what shouldn't be there. Effective writers, as you've seen, work hard at getting their pieces right. The analogy with giving birth is well known. The writer regards every word, every punctuation mark that emerges from his or her mind and is committed to paper as does the proud parent who brings a child into the world. Who among us would willingly erase our own children? Strike them, maybe, to make them over into something more to our liking. But eradicate them altogether? Never!

Yet sometimes an effective writer must cut out some of the ideas or words to which he or she has become most attached. Only a second, objective reader—unafraid, truthful, but kind—will tell you what has to go and why. Contrary to the myths of the publishing profession, effective writers enjoy working with effective editors. Without effective editing, most of what gets into print would be much more sophomoric than modern literature already is.

You don't need to publish your work to have it critiqued. Someone you trust will do. Bob, for example, will give his presentation to Allen to read and edit.

You, in turn, must be open to the feedback you've asked to receive. There's no sense in passing your work on to someone else if you intend to resist suggestions. That doesn't mean you have to take all suggestions to heart. It's still your work, your responsibility to produce what you think is right. Nevertheless, consider the fact that a well-chosen reader has the perspective of the audience for which you are writing. If you hear little applause, change your act or get out of the spotlight.

You have to *talk* to your audience. No matter how well organized and coherent your outline, no matter how well tied together by your thesis sentence, nothing produces understanding except the words you use. Only talking to your audience produces understanding, and to talk to your audience, you have to *"KISS 'em."* (That's an acronym, folks, not an amorous suggestion.)

KISS—"<u>K</u>eep <u>I</u>t <u>S</u>imple and <u>S</u>traightforward"

You've probably heard that as "<u>K</u>eep <u>i</u>t <u>s</u>imple, <u>s</u>tupid," but I don't like calling anyone stupid. Besides, you really do have to keep your written language simple and straightforward. To do that, you have to choose words that everyone in your audience will understand, not just the experts. You have to keep your sentences relatively short and uncluttered. Use the active voice, which I will talk more about in the next section. Use colorful words. If possible, use creative visuals or graphics that illustrate the words.

Save technical jargon for technical talks to technicians. And even then, they may not understand you either. When Einstein published his first major work on relativity, fewer than a dozen people on Earth could read and understand it. And for heaven's sake, don't try to impress anyone with your vocabulary. Ten dollar words aren't worth a dime if no one but you understands them.

Everyday language—that's what everyday people understand. If you must use special or technical words, be sure you define them in some immediate and direct way, even if you have to place footnotes at the bottom of your pages.

The same thing holds true for words with private or culturally defined meanings. What means something to you may not mean much to anyone else. The impact of television, especially of the talk shows, has enriched our language immeasurably by crossing ethnic lines. Words like *chutzpah, macho,* and *paisano* now have meaning for most Americans; however, a Britisher's use of the word *lift* may confound those same people. Language grows and evolves, serving us better as it does.

On the other hand, the growth and evolution of language create problems as well. Older people may not be familiar with newly coined words, such as *quarks* and *quasar.* And words that meant one thing to us when we were young may mean something entirely different to the young today (*gay*, for instance).

Keeping it simple and straightforward means, therefore, finding out something about your audience before you write for it. And if you can't do that, then assume that your audience doesn't know as much about your subject as you do, and make your points clear and unambiguous. Avoid metaphors that are not self-explanatory. Use analogies to clarify unusual situations or events or points. Keep your sentences uncluttered and uncomplicated.

Bob's thesis sentence in the outline had nothing ungrammatical about it, and I didn't rewrite it only to add the "grabber" language. No, I rewrote it because it was too long and too complicated to follow very easily.

Your reader shouldn't have to reread a sentence just to understand it. Write even technical papers to be read only once with complete comprehension.

In ordinary letter writing, simple sentences work best. In books such as this one, compound sentences and complex sentences have to be carefully constructed to convey only one idea at a time—no matter how complicated the idea itself may be.

Conveying ideas—that's what effective writing is all about. That's where I started this discussion many pages ago. Ideas are conveyed more effectively if you use colorful language—language that captures the spirit of the intended meaning as well as its essence. "The sun set" and "The horizon burst into flame as it crossed the face of the setting sun" refer to the same event, but they don't convey the same message.

Poets have no monopoly on colorful language. Anyone can make his or her writing more colorful—first, by reading the work of effective writers, published and/or unpublished, and second, by working on his or her own vocabulary.

Use the Active Voice

As you're working on developing more colorful words, begin thinking in what grammarians call *the active voice*. Straightforward writing without the active voice—well, what more can I say about it than, "Boring"?

The active voice consists of verbs that describe what's going on, what has happened, or what will happen. Look at these two simple examples. First, the passive voice:

The book was read by Mr. Jones.

Wordy, uninteresting writers have little or no impact on their audience. The passive voice is wordy and uninteresting.

Now, the active voice:

Mr. Jones read the book.

The active voice holds the reader's attention. It's descriptive. It tells a story. Coupling the active voice with colorful words has impact, even when you're talking about mundane matters. Another look at Bob's thesis sentence will illustrate my point:

Passive voice: *The income of ABC Foods will be increased by introducing a new adult breakfast cereal.*

Now compare that with the following, a straightforward (no-hype) rewrite of the passive-voiced sentence above:

Active voice: *By introducing a new adult breakfast cereal, ABC Foods will increase its revenues by 20 percent.*

If Bob said he had to use one of those two sentences and asked you which he should choose, which would you suggest? Silly question, isn't it? The sentence in the active voice, with a strong verb and a measurable goal, will definitely grab the board of directors much faster and much more firmly than will the one in the passive voice.

The choice of words and the use of the active voice are what most people mean when they say that so-and-so writes with style. When I talk about writing style, I also mean the form that the writing takes. I've been talking about expository writing, the writing that most of us have to do on a regular basis. The narrative style, the other most frequently used style, makes different demands on the writer than does exposition.

Narration and Description

The *narrative* tells a story. It describes people, places, events, or things. What I called a thesis sentence earlier, I now call a theme. It refers to the point of the story, the universal element in it with which anyone reading it can identify.

The story of a narrative is called a plot—even if you're writing nonfiction. You build the outline of the plot from a series of incidents that lead to events. The first and most important incident is called the "precipitating event." It's what sets the whole chain of events into motion. Here chronology plays a larger role than it did in selecting the order of an expository outline, although you still need to consider the other principles of selection: importance, meaning, value, impact, and logic.

Narratives, as noted above, are usually used to *describe* events, people, places, or things rather than to explain something. To describe people, a special form of outline called a character sketch is used. For each person in the story, you develop one sketch, which includes every characteristic or trait about the person that is relevant or pertinent to the story and to his or her relationships with other characters and/or events.

Effective narrative writers develop their prose style to the quality of poetry. Not only fiction writers but essayists as well take command of their audiences by the power of their words. But what about you? Am I expecting you to become a world-renowned essayist merely by reading this book?

Hardly. But on the other hand, the next time you sit down to write a letter to your school chum who moved across the country, think how much more he or she will enjoy reading your letter if you talk in an exciting narrative form. You can put an end to the babbling and rambling I mentioned at the beginning of this book if you'll take a moment to think through what you're about to say in print. Write an outline, character sketches, too, if you will. At least develop a few notes to tell yourself where you're going with this letter (its purpose, your point and/or your point of view).

Polish

Polish consists of changing a word here, a phrase there to make the reader remember what you've said. It also consists of the transitions that you write between ideas.

Paragraphs linked together by a common content fill endless columns on the pages of daily newspapers, but ordinary boilerplate rarely makes for exciting reading. Feature columns, on the other hand, usually do grab and hold your attention, partly because more than common content holds the paragraphs together.

The glue that holds the whole piece together is called transitions: words, phrases, or sentences that connect one paragraph to another. The immediately preceding sentence is not only the topic sentence of this paragraph; it's the transition between this paragraph and the one above. It connects the idea of polishing your writing with one method of doing it: writing transitions and what transitions are.

Chapter 7

How to Write Letters and Memos That Really Get Your Point Across

If writing in general is talking on paper, then writing letters and memos in particular clearly represents your own voice. They're true extensions of yourself because, when written well, they make people look forward to hearing more from you. When written badly, they turn people off and become barriers to further dealings. Whether you're writing to clients, to other companies, to other departments, to superiors, or to subordinates, your letters or memos are your voice. They're what people know you by.

To speak well in letters or memos, know your purpose before you begin to write; identify your point or theme in the very beginning (obeying the "Tell 'em" principle). Be brief, choosing your words carefully and economically. Control your tone by recognizing your point of view and conveying the point of view best suited to get the proper response, the response appropriate to the theme.

"I haven't got all day. Get to the point." That's what busy people say if they read a letter or memo that beats around the bush or states its theme fuzzily. Put yourself in your reader's shoes. Use the "Tell 'em" principle to get to the point in the first sentence, stating your thesis or conclusion up front, to give the reader a reason to continue, before developing your case.

Then remember, when developing your case, that the reader really hasn't got all day. Keep it brief. KISS works here, too. Keep it simple and straightforward. Choose the right words to communicate your ideas, using the grandma test, if you can, to ensure that you've gotten your point across.

But in your zeal to be brief, avoid terseness. Your tone of voice can turn off someone you want to keep as a friend or an ally even if you're rejecting him or her as an employee or as a co-worker. The reader's self-esteem should be considered by asking, "How would I feel if I received this letter?"

For example, compare "Your proposal to change accounting systems has been rejected" with "Though your proposal to change accounting systems has genuine merit, because of a lack of personnel to make the change, we will not be able to adopt the proposal at this time." Though the second statement is longer and says more than the first, it conveys to the reader what he or she needs to know.

Choosing the right words helps convey tone of voice. Goods are "inexpensive" rather than "cheap." "Superb" may exaggerate when "good" will suffice. "ASAP" is vague, whereas "tomorrow" sets a deadline the reader can understand. The right words in a thoroughgoing sentence communicate clearly and concisely.

Letters and memos may be alike in content or purpose, but they differ from each other in special ways.

Letters

Unless you're writing a note to a friend, letters are more formal than memos. Letters leave the premises—they're sent out the door with a postage stamp on the envelope. Memos stay inside.

Letters usually are personal and confidential, even if the content is common knowledge. That personal touch is captured in the format—for example, "Dear Mr. Smith"—illustrated in the accompanying sidebar.

Every letter requires a return address (even if you don't use a letterhead), the date, the recipient's address, a greeting or salutation, the body of the letter, an appropriate close, your signature, and if needed, special notations (for example, for copies or enclosures).

How well you know the recipient, his or her position or status, and the purpose of the letter dictate the greeting or salutation. "Dear Jerry" is appropriate for someone you know well, even if the purpose of the letter is more formal than that. However, in most business letters, especially when you're requesting something of a person in a relatively important position, Mr., Mrs., or Ms. works best.

The methods I've already described—jotting down notes, combining those notes into an orderly outline, fleshing out the outline into a first draft, revising the draft—all apply to writing the body of a letter, regardless of the letter's purpose.

Purpose dictates content and order. What you want from the other person or what you have to offer or what you have to communicate structures the letter itself. In the example, Ms. Jones wants to remind Mr. Smith that he owes the company for the shipment of goods that he denies having received even though he signed for the goods on the shipping order. Any other letter, with any other purpose, begins with the same message: This is what the letter is about.

Letter

Honey Comb Company
555 Main Street
Anywhere, Any State 11111
June 1, 1986

Mr. George Smith
Hard Goods Retail Stores
234 Central Avenue
Small Town, Small State 22222

Dear Mr. Smith:

Please be kind enough to pay the amount shown on the copy of the invoice enclosed. As you know, our terms are net 10 days, and our records show that it has now been 60 days since delivery was made.

We acknowledge your claim that you never received the shipment, and we have checked with the carrier, whose records confirm ours that delivery of the 100 Honey Comb units took place on April 1, 1986. Your signature on the invoice, on the "Received by" line, matches your signature on other correspondence. Therefore, please correct your records and make your payment immediately.

Mr. Smith, we value your business and want to continue doing business with you. We hope that once this minor confusion is ironed out, we will hear from you again whenever your supply of Honey Combs runs out.

Sincerely,

Sally Jones

Sally Jones, Supervisor
Accounts Receivable

cc: John Doe, President
Encl: Invoice #6667

Memos

Memos differ in tone of voice, purpose, and structure from letters, but they, too, must follow the "Tell 'em" principle and use the KISS approach. Whether a hastily scribbled note to a co-worker about a lunch meeting or a formal statement of policy, memos are designed for in-house use, and though distributed narrowly, their subjects are not usually personal or confidential. When they are, a sealed envelope marked "personal" and/or "confidential" is in order.

Memo

TO: Allen Friendly, Manager
                Shipping Department

FROM: Bill Thomas, President   BT

DATE: June 1, 1986

SUBJECT: Routine shipments

Effective immediately, please have your personnel stamp the word "Routine" on all invoices of shipments made on standing orders. This will alert the Billing Department to calendar the bills on the dates assigned to each customer.

I appreciate your help with this, Allen, because there's been some confusion with the billings to regular customers. The new computerized billing procedure will eliminate that problem only if the Billing Department knows which orders are routine and which are special. This procedure should help.

Thanks.

BT

Memos, such as the example in the accompanying sidebar, form the basis of internal business communication and should be uniform in style no matter what the content: notice of a meeting, statement of policy, statement of facts or figures, reports, clarifications, and so on. They start off with the name of the recipient, the name of the sender, the date, and a brief subject heading and are followed by the body.

Most organizations have done away with the signature, replacing it with the sender's initials at the end. In a typewritten memo, such as the one shown in the example, the sender initials the heading to show that he or she has read the memo and that it says what was intended.

The most serious flaw in office memos is usually tone of voice. Office memos often read like orations or technical manuals. Speak on paper the same way you would speak out loud to the recipient(s). Remember, you work *together*—you're colleagues and friends. Talk to these people on paper the way you'd talk to any other friends in person.

Chapter 8

Conclusion

This is where I tell you what I told you. This is the summary.

Everyone writes. At one time or another, each of us writes notes to the children, or letters to parents, or memos to co-workers, or presentations to the board of directors. Some people simply write more effectively than others, and those who get their work published are called "authors."

Effective writing is organized, coherent talking. All writing, I've said, is talking on paper. When writing, you send your messages through your hand rather than through your mouth. While writing, subvocalizing (speaking silently) helps make your message easier to communicate, and that's what writing is all about: communicating a message by representing sounds with printed words.

After writing, read your piece aloud to smooth out the rough spots. Give it the "grandma test," by having a trusted friend read it for you and give you feedback. When writing, you're in complete control over your words. If they fail to say what you intend, you have only yourself to blame for having reworked the piece inadequately.

Effective writers make their point clear and unambiguous, stating their purpose up front and explaining their main point (thesis, theme) and point of view. They use ordinary language—language their audiences can understand. They write in their own style, and they keep that style simple and straightforward (KISS), using active, colorful words in uncomplicated, easy-to-comprehend sentences.

But most important of all, effective writing requires that you take the jumble of rough ideas with which you start and put them together into a logical and/or chronological order. You outline your ideas, in a topic outline or a sentence outline (or both). You draw your main point (for example, your thesis) out of your purpose for writing in the first place.

Any kind of writing—a letter, a memo, a report, a speech, or a book—is talking on paper. The formats vary, but the steps I've developed will help you write anything, whether it be a formal essay or an informal letter. In fact, an easy rule to follow is that almost all effective writing (even fiction) is really a letter—a communication between the writer and the reader.

Suggested Readings

Your memos, letters, and reports will benefit from your familiarity with the following:

Holcombe, Marya W., and Stein, Judith K. *Writing for Decision Makers: Memos and Reports with a Competitive Edge.* Belmont, Calif.: Lifetime Learning Publications, 1981.

Roddick, Ellen. *Writing That Means Business: A Manager's Guide.* New York: Macmillan, 1984.

Roman, Kenneth, and Raphaelson, Joel. *Writing that Works: How to Write Memos, Letters, Reports, Speeches, Resumés, Plans and Other Papers That Say What You Mean—And Get Things Done.* New York: Harper & Row, 1981.

Strunk, William, Jr., and White, E. B. *The Elements of Style.* New York: Macmillan, 1959.

Index

About the Author

Donald H. Weiss is an Account Executive for Psychological Associates, a training and development company, and President of Self-Management Associates, a small-business consulting firm located in Dallas. Along with the six books in the Successful Office Skills series, he has written numerous books, articles, video scripts, and study guides on business management and related topics. Dr. Weiss is the author of AMACOM's popular cassette/workbook programs *Getting Results, How to Manage for Higher Productivity,* and *Managing Conflict.*

Dr. Weiss holds a Ph.D. in social theory from Tulane University, as well as degrees from the University of Arizona and the University of Missouri. He has also taught at several colleges and universities. He is a member of the American Society for Training and Development.